# CRIME MOVIE POS

volume five of
the illustrated history of movies through posters

Images from the Hershenson-Allen Archive

Published by BRUCE HERSHENSON
P.O. Box 874, West Plains, MO 65775
(417) 256-9616 (phone) • (417) 257-6948 (fax)

## ABOUT THE HERSHENSON-ALLEN ARCHIVE

Bruce Hershenson has published thirteen books containing movie poster images. His archive, Bruce Hershenson Archive, contains poster images from over fifteen thousand different films, as well as tens of thousands of film pressbooks. He has organized ten auctions of original movie posters at Christie's, the world-famous auction house, that cumulatively have taken in just under ten million dollars.

Richard Allen has for many years been one of the world's foremost collectors of movie posters. His archive, The Carson Collection, contains a huge percentage of the finest poster images known to exist. The Carson Collection was the primary source of images for Reel Art, selected as one of the hundred best film books ever made, and for Chronicles of the Cinema, which contains over one thousand poster images, as well as numerous other film books.

In 1997, after joining forces on three books, the Bruce Hershenson Archive and The Carson Collection have merged into the Hershenson-Allen Archive. The combined archive will continue to provide images for film books, magazines, video cassettes, and much more. All of the images in the archive are photographed directly from the original posters on the highest quality four by five transparencies. Anyone wishing further information should contact:

Hershenson-Allen Archive
812 West Broadway
West Plains, MO 65775
phone (417) 256-9616
fax (417) 257-6948

# INTRODUCTION

Welcome to the fifth volume of **The Illustrated History of Movies Through Posters.** Volume One in the series is **Cartoon Movie Posters**, Volume Two is **Cowboy Movie Posters**, Volume Three is **Academy Award Winners' Movie Posters**, and Volume Four is **Sports Movie Posters**. The sixth and seventh volumes will be **Horror Movie Posters** and **More Cowboy Movie Posters**.

This book is an overview of the thousands of films that have been made that have an aspect of crime as their central theme. Because of space limitations, only a small percentage of those films could be included in this book, and many difficult choices had to be made. First and foremost, of course, posters must exist from a film for it to be included. This explains why there are very few posters from silent films or from the many pre-Rathbone Sherlock Holmes films, for example. Another reason posters might be excluded is because the film can be reasonably included in another genre (such as The Man Who Shot Liberty Valence or The Count of Monte Cristo). If a film seemed marginally a crime film, it was left out of the book.

There are a few areas of crime films which I excluded solely because of space limitations. The first is spy films, which could fill an entire volume of their own, especially the James Bond series. The second is thrillers that seem to be as much about horror as crime (with the notable exception being Psycho, which I couldn't bear to leave out). The third is courtroom dramas that focus primarily on a trial, such as Inherit the Wind (although I included My Cousin Vinny, which is both a courtroom film and a comedy, just because I love the movie so much). Two areas which could have been excluded, but I chose not to, are prison movies (because they are such personal favorites) and "bad girl" films, because so often the films have great images and taglines.

I found that once I included all the most memorable films, and all the posters with sensational graphics, there was little room for anything else. I have tried to include at least some posters from all the years of sound films, to best show the continuing development of crime movies and their poster art. I confess to including many personal favorites, and I am well aware that many worthy films do not appear. But that is what follow-up volumes are for. I welcome any suggestions as to posters you would like included in the eventual sequel. If you own a striking poster that you believe to be rare and would be willing to have it pictured in a follow-up volume, please contact me.

Unless otherwise indicated, all of the illustrations are of the original United States release one-sheet poster (41"x27"). Other sizes included are lobby cards (11"x14"), window cards (14"x22"), inserts (14"x36"), half-sheets (22"x28"), three-sheets (81"x41"), and six-sheets (81"x81"), and foreign posters (varying sizes). **This is not a catalog of posters for sale, nor do I sell reproductions.** However, I do sell vintage movie posters of all sorts, both through sales catalogs and auctions. If you are interested in acquiring posters, or if you want to purchase past volumes of this series (or any of the other books I have published), please contact me.

If this books looks better than other picture books, it is because of the talents of those who assembled it. Sylvia Hershenson brought together the written material, and did the proofreading. Many of the posters were photographed by David Graveen. The book was printed by Courier Graphics, under the guidance of Ginger Dickinson.

I wish to dedicate this book to the memory of my dear friend, Barry Bauman (1947-1997). We met as teenagers and instantly became close friends. Our friendship lasted thirty years, and some of my happiest memories are of times I spent with Barry. He is missed.

- Bruce Hershenson
West Plains, Missouri
September 1997

Note: The subject of crime movies is so broad that numerous books have been written about various sub-genres, including film noir, Hitchcock and so on. This book does not attempt to discuss the movies themselves. If the reader wishes to learn more about specific films, he is urged to consult any of the many fine reference works available. The intent of this book is to present the most important and striking original crime movie posters known to exist, more than one might hope to find in the most lavish coffee table book. All posters were photographed directly from the originals, and this book was printed using the finest technology available. Note that the posters are presented in fairly strict chronological order, except for the series films, which are grouped together, to better present the evolution of the films and posters.

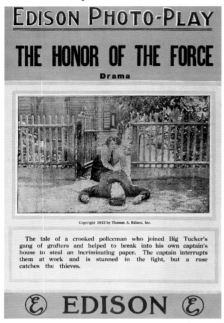

1 THE HONOR OF THE FORCE, 1913

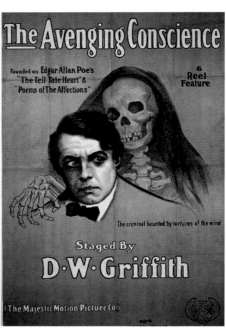

2 THE AVENGING CONSCIENCE, 1914

3 THE CYPHER MESSAGE, 1913

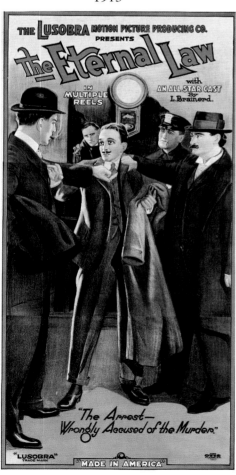

4 THE ETERNAL LAW, c.1910, three-sheet

5 LIFE IN JOLIET PENITENTIARY, c.1910, three-sheet

6 WHO'S GUILTY?, 1916, three-sheet

7 THE THIRD DEGREE, 1913

8 THE GIRL, THE COP,
THE BURGLAR, 1914

9 THE TONGUE MARK, 1913

10 TRAFFIC IN SOULS, 1913

11 THE PERILS OF PAULINE, 1914

12 THE HOODLUM, 1919

13 THE PENALTY, 1920

14 VELVET FINGERS, 1921,
three-sheet

15 OUTSIDE THE LAW, 1921

16 OUTSIDE THE LAW, 1921

17 THE AMATEUR DETECTIVE, 1925

18 THE UNHOLY THREE, 1925

19 UNDERWORLD, 1927

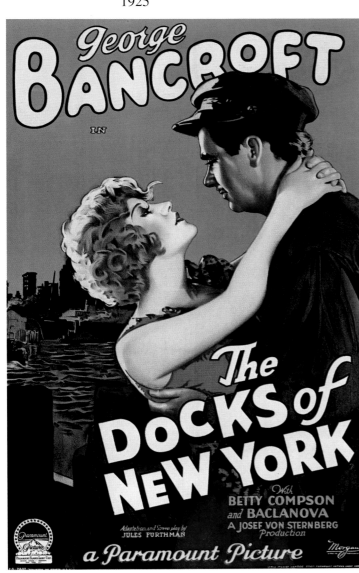

20 THE DOCKS OF NEW YORK, 1928

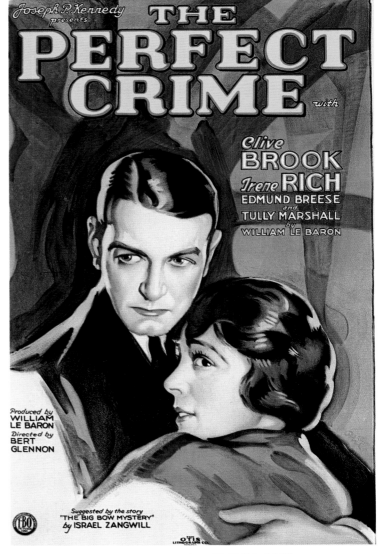

21 THE PERFECT CRIME, 1928

22 SHERLOCK HOLMES, 1922, lobby card set

23 MORIARTY, 1922

24 SHERLOCK HOLMES, 1922, six-sheet

25 THE SIGN OF FOUR,
1924, Australian daybill

26 THE RETURN OF
SHERLOCK HOLMES 1929, insert

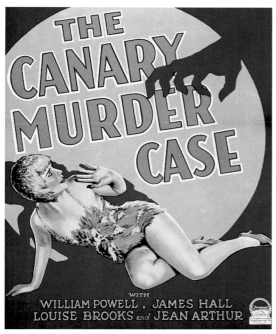

27 THE CANARY MURDER CASE, 1929, window card

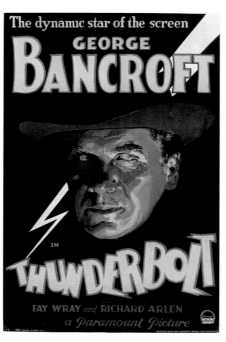

28 THUNDERBOLT, 1929

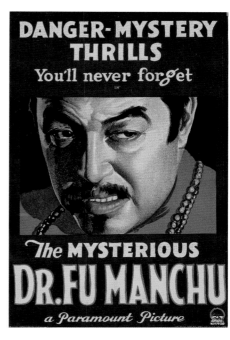

29 THE MYSTERIOUS DR. FU MANCHU, 1929

30 THE GREENE MURDER CASE, 1929, insert

31 BLACKMAIL, 1929, Australian daybill

32 BULLDOG DRUMMOND, 1929, three-sheet

34 RAFFLES, 1930, lobby card

33 THE WOMAN WHO NEEDED KILLING,
1929, window card

35 SINNERS' HOLIDAY, 1930, lobby card

36 THE DOORWAY TO HELL, 1930

37 THE UNHOLY THREE, 1930, lobby card

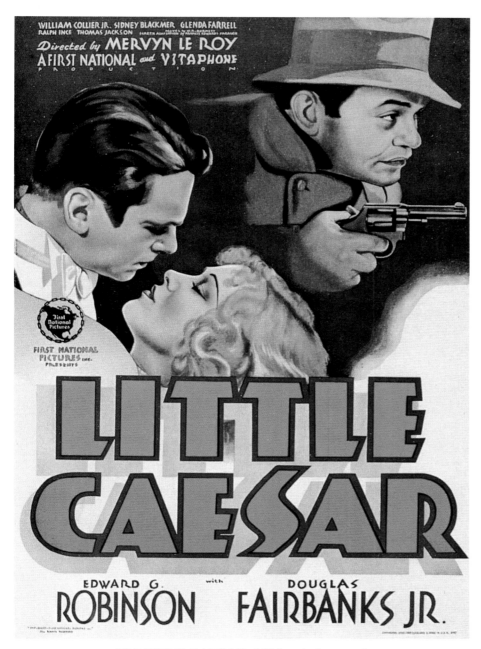

38 LITTLE CAESAR, 1930, window card

39 THE PUBLIC ENEMY, 1931, insert

Note: 1930 was an extremely important year in the evolution of American crime films. Little Caesar was the first major film to glorify a gangster (even though he dies at the end of the film). The huge success of this film quickly brought on a slew of similar films, including Public Enemy and Scarface, as well as scores of less talented productions. 1930 was also the year Sinner's Holiday was made. The film marked the debuts of both James Cagney and an unbilled Joan Blondell. Neither were pictured on the film's poster art, but both are prominent on one memorable lobby card.

40 PUBLIC ENEMY, 1931, lobby card

41 THE BLACK CAMEL, 1931

42 CHARLIE CHAN'S CHANCE, 1932

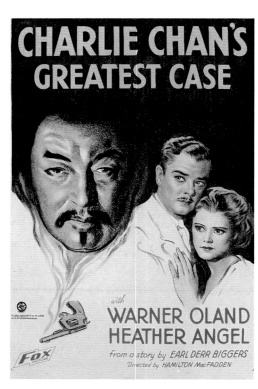

43 CHARLIE CHAN'S GREATEST
CASE, 1933

44 CHARLIE CHAN IN
SHANGHAI, 1935, three-sheet

45 CHARLIE CHAN AT THE CIRCUS,
1936

46 CHARLIE CHAN AT THE OPERA, 1936

47 CHARLIE CHAN AT MONTE CARLO, 1937

Note: Warner Oland did not originate the role of Charlie Chan, but he was the most successful of those who played the character. Furthermore, the Oland films were made for Fox (later Twentieth Century Fox) which created striking posters for every film. After Oland's death in 1937, more Chan films were made (#128-142).

48 CHARLIE CHAN AT THE OLYMPICS, 1937

49 CHARLIE CHAN ON BROADWAY, 1937

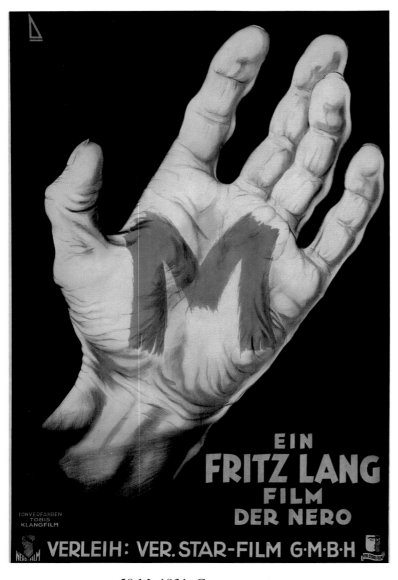

50 M, 1931, German poster

51 GUILTY AS HELL, 1932

Note: M, an incredible German film, had a huge influence on American crime films of the 1930s. Its star, Peter Lorre, and director, Fritz Lang, would later emigrate to the United States and make many memorable films.

52 THE SILENT WITNESS, 1932

53 ARSENE LUPIN, 1932, lobby card

54 THE STRANGE CASE OF
CLARA DEANE, 1932

55 TROUBLE IN PARADISE, 1932, campaign book ad

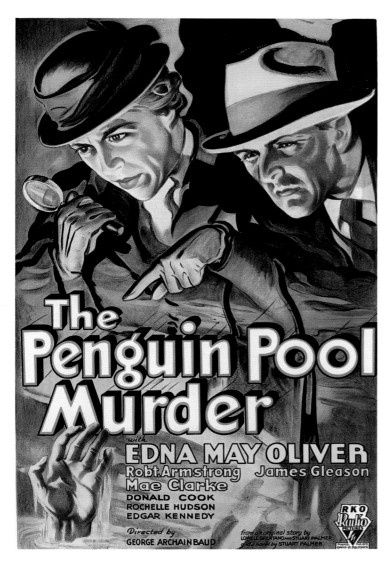

56 THE PENGUIN POOL MURDER, 1932

57 JEWEL ROBBERY, 1932

58 I AM A FUGITIVE FROM A CHAIN GANG, 1932,
lobby card

59 I AM A FUGITIVE FROM A CHAIN GANG, 1932,
lobby card

60 I AM A FUGITIVE FROM A CHAIN GANG, 1932,
Argentinian poster

61 SCARFACE, 1932, lobby card

62 SCARFACE, 1937 reissue

63 BLONDIE JOHNSON, 1933

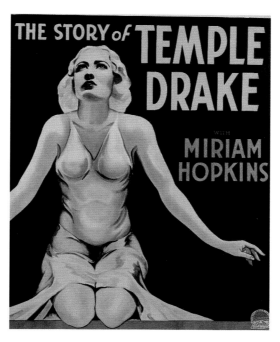

64 THE STORY OF TEMPLE DRAKE, 1933, window card

65 THE CIRCUS QUEEN MURDER, 1933

66 LADY KILLER, 1933

67 LADIES THEY TALK ABOUT, 1933

68 THE LITTLE GIANT, 1933

69 THE CRIME DOCTOR, 1934

70 THE SIN OF NORA MORAN, 1934

Note: William Powell and Myrna Loy were overshadowed by Clark Gable in Manhattan Melodrama, but they will be forever remembered for The Thin Man series of films.

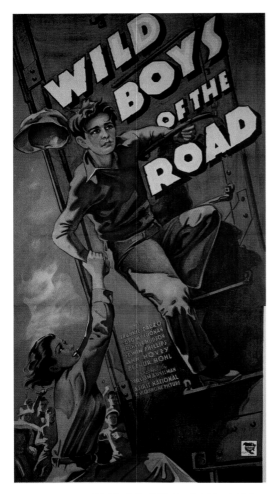

71 WILD BOYS OF THE ROAD, 1933, three-sheet

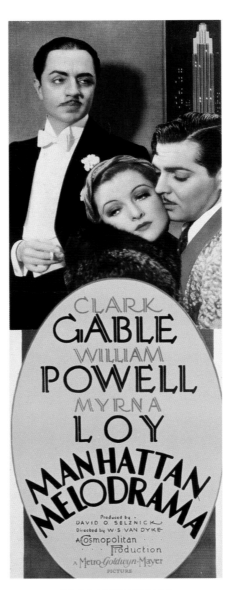

72 MANHATTAN MELODRAMA, 1934, insert

73 MILLION DOLLAR RANSOM, 1934, three-sheet

74 THE THIN MAN, 1934

75 AFTER THE THIN MAN, 1936

76 SHADOW OF THE THIN MAN,
1941

77 THE THIN MAN GOES HOME,
1944

78 SONG OF THE THIN MAN,
1947

79 G-MEN, 1935, three-sheet

80 THE INFORMER, 1935, three-sheet

81 STAR OF MIDNIGHT, 1935, three-sheet

82 BORDERTOWN 1935

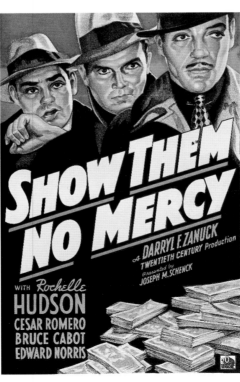

83 SHOW THEM NO MERCY, 1935

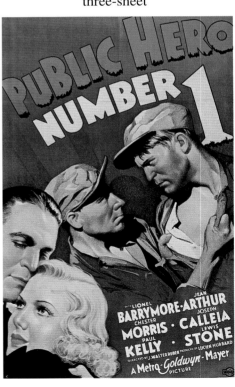

84 PUBLIC HERO NUMBER 1, 1935

85 MYSTERIOUS MR. WONG, 1935

86 THE MYSTERY OF MR. WONG, 1938, lobby card

87 MR. WONG, DETECTIVE, 1938

88 MR. WONG IN CHINATOWN, 1939, lobby card

89 PHANTOM OF CHINATOWN, 1940, lobby card

90 BLACK LEGION, 1936

91 SATAN MET A LADY, 1936, insert

92 THE CASE OF THE BLACK CAT, 1936

93 THE PETRIFIED FOREST, 1936, three-sheet

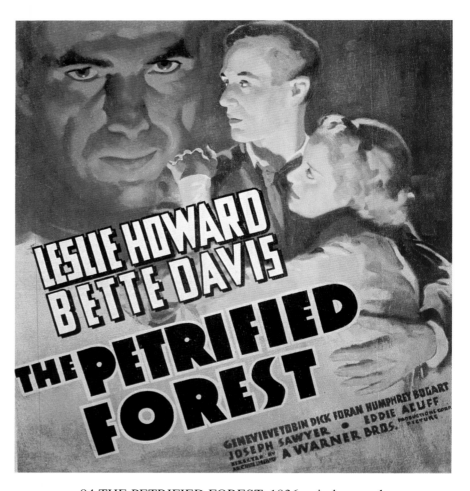

94 THE PETRIFIED FOREST, 1936, window card

95 THE LEAGUE OF FRIGHTENED MEN, 1937

96 UNDERWORLD, 1937

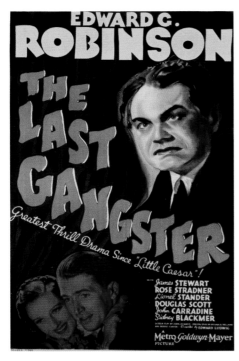

97 THE LAST GANGSTER, 1937

98 MARKED WOMAN, 1937, lobby card

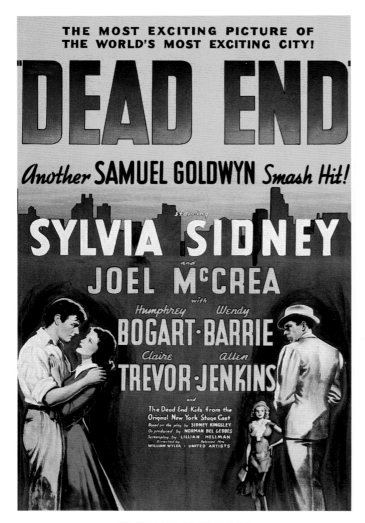

99 DEAD END, 1937

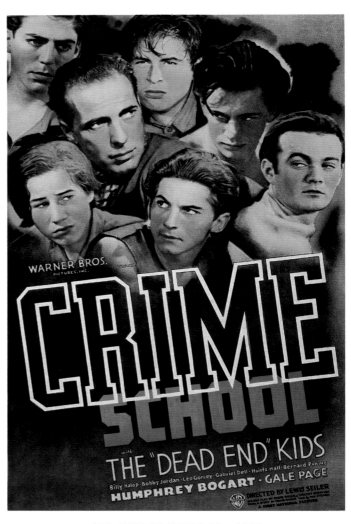

100 CRIME SCHOOL, 1938

101 DEAD END, 1937, lobby card

102 CRIME SCHOOL,
1938, insert

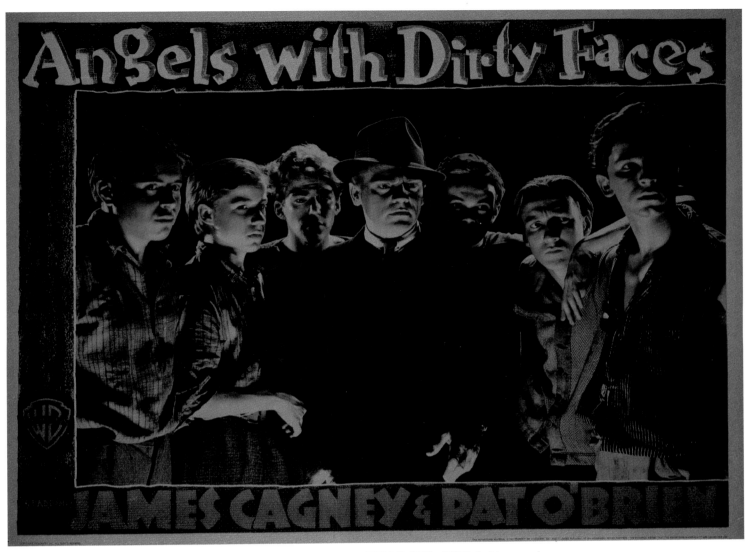

103 ANGELS WITH DIRTY FACES, 1938, lobby card

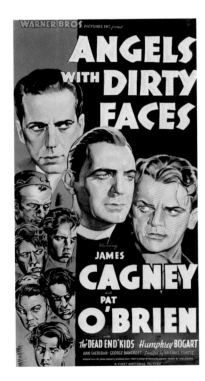

104 ANGELS WITH DIRTY
FACES, 1938, three-sheet

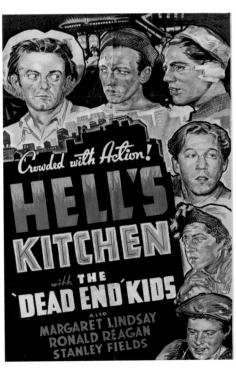

105 HELL'S KITCHEN, 1939, "other
company"

106 THEY MADE ME A CRIMINAL,
1939

107 DICK TRACY, 1937

108 DICK TRACY, 1937

109 DICK TRACY, 1945

Dick Tracy was first filmed as a serial in 1937. The one-sheets from the individual chapters are prized for the Chester Gould comic strip art.

110 DICK TRACY VS. CUEBALL, 1946, lobby card

111 DICK TRACY'S DILEMMA, 1947

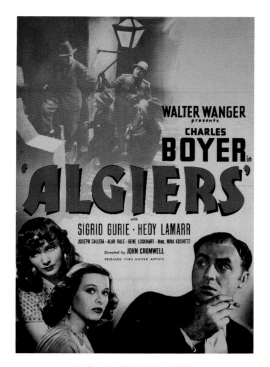

112 ALGIERS, 1938

113 WANTED BY THE POLICE, 1938

114 MYSTERIOUS MR. MOTO, 1938

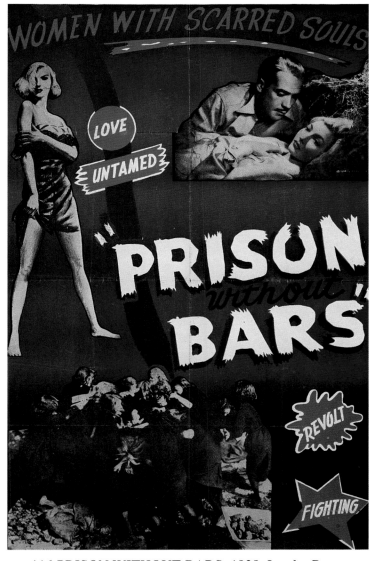

115 THE AMAZING DR. CLITTERHOUSE, 1938, "other company"

116 PRISON WITHOUT BARS, 1938, Leader Press

117 THE SAINT IN NEW YORK, 1938

118 THE SAINT STRIKES BACK, 1939, lobby card

119 THE SAINT IN PALM SPRINGS, 1941, lobby card

120 THE SAINT'S VACATION, 1941, lobby card

121 THE SAINT MEETS THE TIGER, 1943

122 THE ROARING TWENTIES, 1939, insert

123 KING OF THE UNDERWORLD, 1939, insert

124 KING OF CHINATOWN, 1939, three-sheet

125 YOU CAN'T GET AWAY WITH MURDER, 1939

126 EACH DAWN I DIE, 1939, jumbo window card

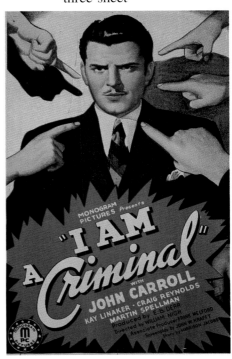

127 I AM A CRIMINAL, 1939

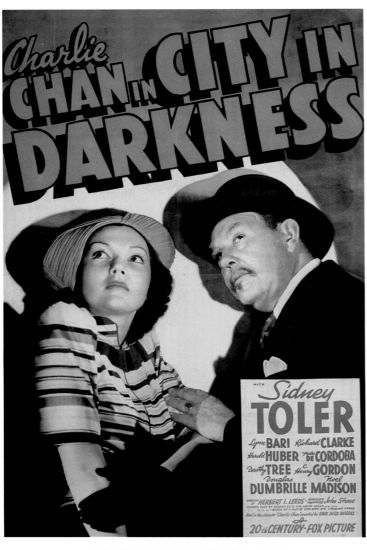

128 CITY IN DARKNESS, 1939

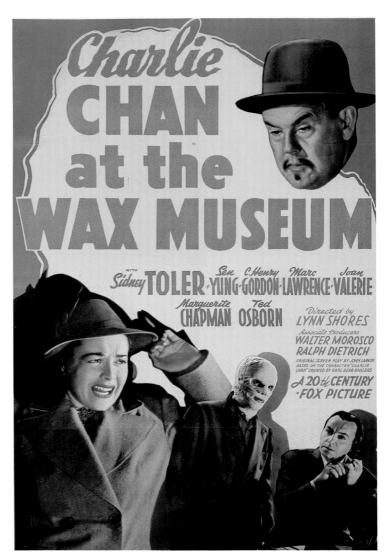

129 CHARLIE CHAN AT THE WAX MUSEUM, 1940

130 CHARLIE CHAN IN THE SECRET SERVICE, 1944

131 THE CHINESE CAT, 1944

132 BLACK MAGIC, 1944

133 THE SHANGHAI COBRA, 1945, lobby card

134 THE RED DRAGON, 1945, lobby card

135 DANGEROUS MONEY, 1946, lobby card

136 DARK ALIBI, 1946, lobby card

137 THE TRAP, 1947, lobby card

138 THE CHINESE RING, 1947, lobby card

139 DOCKS OF NEW ORLEANS, 1948, lobby card

140 THE SHANGHAI CHEST, 1948, lobby card

141 THE FEATHERED SERPENT, 1948, lobby card

142 SKY DRAGON, 1948, lobby card

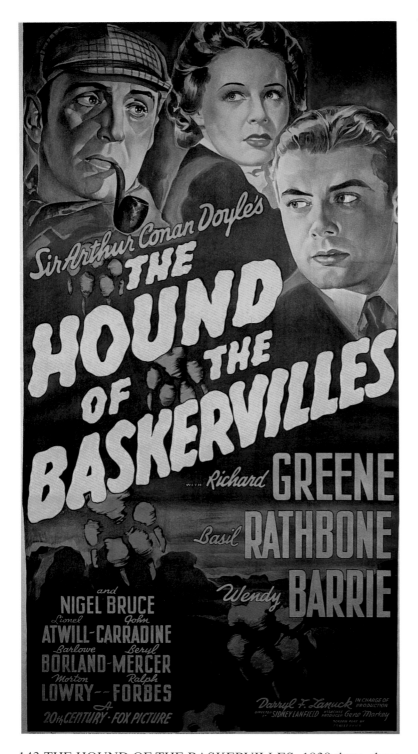

143 THE HOUND OF THE BASKERVILLES, 1939,three-sheet

Note: While there were a surprisingly large number of Holmes films prior to 1939, The Hound of the Baskervilles was a huge success, and established Rathbone as the definitive Sherlock Holmes. The film was so successful that Twentieth Century Fox rushed out a sequel the same year.

144 THE ADVENTURES OF SHERLOCK HOLMES, 1939, insert

145 SHERLOCK HOLMES AND THE
SECRET WEAPON, 1942

146 SHERLOCK HOLMES AND THE VOICE OF TERROR,
1942, lobby card

147 SHERLOCK HOLMES IN WASHINGTON, 1943

148 SHERLOCK HOLMES FACES DEATH, 1943

149 THE SCARLET CLAW, 1944

150 SPIDER WOMAN, 1944, lobby card

151 THE HOUSE OF FEAR, 1945,
lobby card

152 TERROR BY NIGHT, 1946,
lobby card

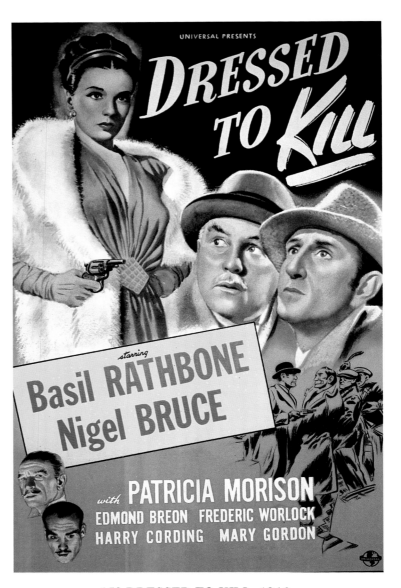

153 DRESSED TO KILL, 1946

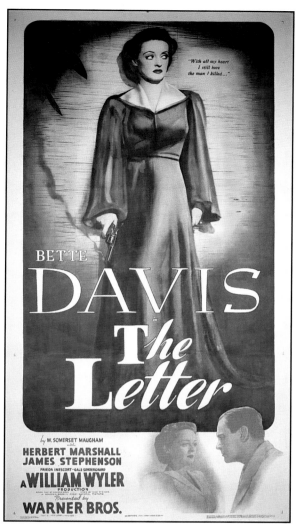

154 THE LETTER, 1940, three-sheet

155 THE MALTESE FALCON, 1941, window card

156 BROTHER ORCHID, 1940

157 OUT OF THE FOG, 1941

158 HIGH SIERRA, 1941

159 THE GAY FALCON, 1941, lobby card

160 THE FALCON'S BROTHER, 1942, lobby card

161 THE FALCON TAKES OVER, 1942, lobby card

162 THE FALCON STRIKES BACK, 1943, lobby card

163 THE FALCON AND THE CO-EDS, 1943

164 THE FALCON IN DANGER, 1943

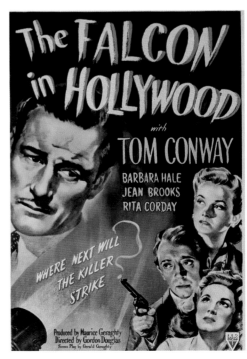

165 THE FALCON IN HOLLYWOOD, 1944

166 THE FALCON IN MEXICO, 1944

167 THE FALCON OUT WEST, 1944

Note: George Sanders had already made several films as The Saint when he began starring as The Falcon in a new series. He tired of that role as well, but rather than simply recast the part, RKO cleverly had his character's brother assume the lead (played by Tom Conway, Sanders' real life brother).

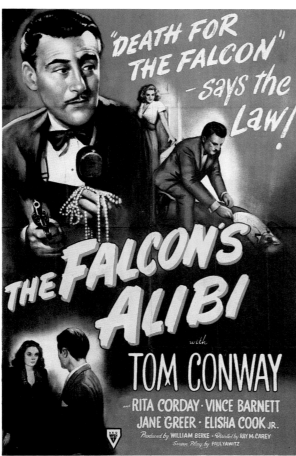

168 THE FALCON'S ALIBI, 1946

169 THE DEVIL'S CARGO, 1948

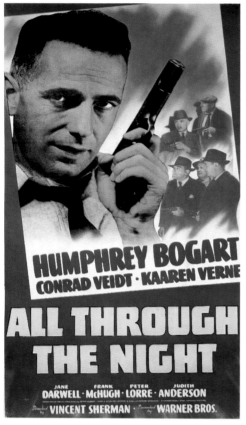

170 ALL THROUGH THE NIGHT,
1942, three-sheet

171 JUKE GIRL, 1942,
three-sheet

172 THE GLASS KEY, 1942, three-
sheet

173 THIS GUN FOR HIRE, 1942

174 CASABLANCA, 1942, six-sheet

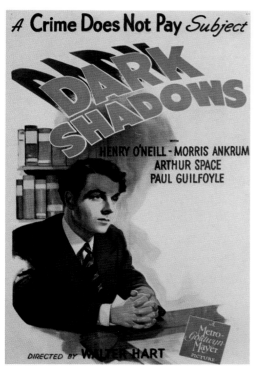

175 DARK SHADOWS, 1942

176 BOSTON BLACKIE GOES HOLLYWOOD, 1942

177 QUIET PLEASE, MURDER, 1942

178 SHADOW OF A DOUBT, 1943

179 MR. LUCKY, 1943, lobby card

180 MINISTRY OF FEAR, 1944, lobby card

181 LADY IN THE DEATH HOUSE, 1944

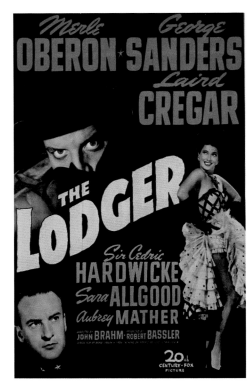

182 THE LODGER, 1944

183 GASLIGHT, 1944

184 LAURA, 1944, three-sheet

185 DOUBLE INDEMNITY, 1944, three-sheet

186 MURDER, MY SWEET, 1944, three-sheet

187 THE WOMAN IN THE WINDOW, 1944, lobby card

188 DETOUR, 1945, lobby card

189 DILLINGER, 1945

190 LEAVE HER TO HEAVEN, 1945

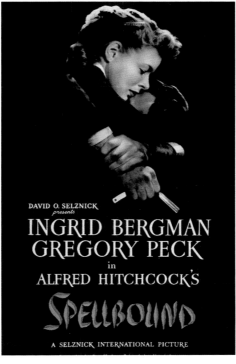

191 SPELLBOUND, 1945

192 SCARLET STREET, 1945

193 NOTORIOUS, 1946

194 THE BLUE DAHLIA, 1946

195 LADY IN THE LAKE, 1946

196 THE KILLERS, 1946

197 THE BIG SLEEP, 1946

198 THE STRANGE LOVE OF
MARTHA IVERS, 1946

199 THE STRANGE LOVE OF MARTHA IVERS, 1946, lobby card

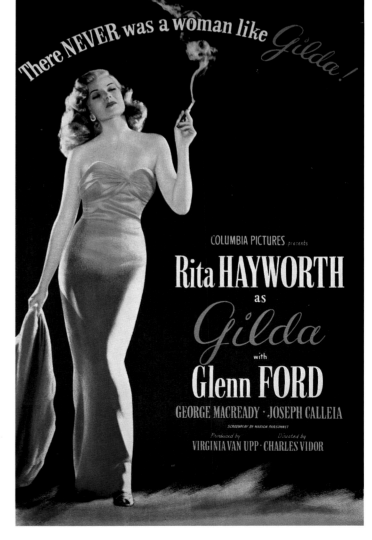

200 THE POSTMAN ALWAYS RINGS TWICE, 1946

201 GILDA, 1946

202 DARK PASSAGE, 1947, six-sheet

203 OUT OF THE PAST, 1947

204 DEAD RECKONING, 1947

205 CROSSFIRE, 1947

206 I WALK ALONE, 1947

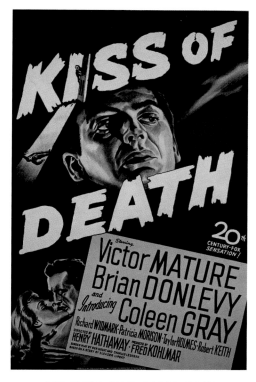

207 KISS OF DEATH, 1947

208 THE DEVIL THUMBS A RIDE, 1947

209 BORN TO KILL, 1947

210 THEY WON'T BELIEVE ME, 1947, lobby card

211 NAKED CITY 1948, lobby card

212 CRY MURDER, 1947, lobby card

213 SECRET BEYOND THE DOOR, 1948, lobby card

214 FORCE OF EVIL, 1948

215 ROPE, 1948

216 KEY LARGO, 1948

217 I LOVE TROUBLE, 1948

218 THE LADY FROM SHANGHAI, 1948

219 INNER SANCTUM MYSTERY, 1948

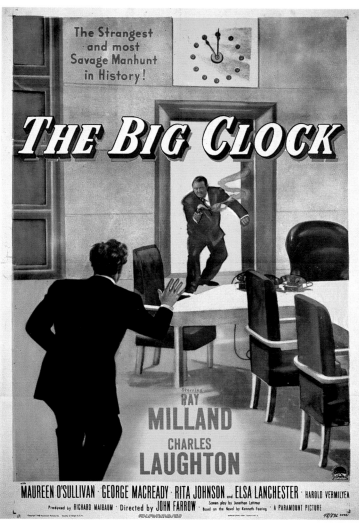

220 THE BIG CLOCK, 1948

221 SORRY WRONG NUMBER,
1948

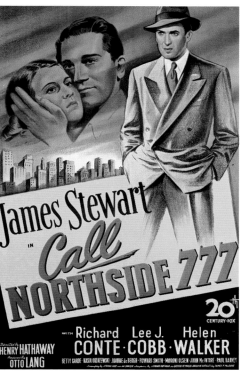

222 CALL NORTHSIDE 777, 1948

223 THE WINDOW, 1949

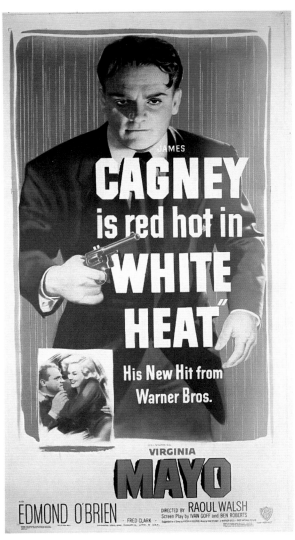

224 THEY LIVE BY NIGHT, 1949

225 WHITE HEAT, 1949, three-sheet

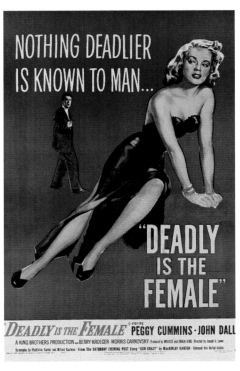

226 TOO LATE FOR TEARS, 1949

227 DEADLY IS THE FEMALE, 1949

228 TRAPPED, 1949

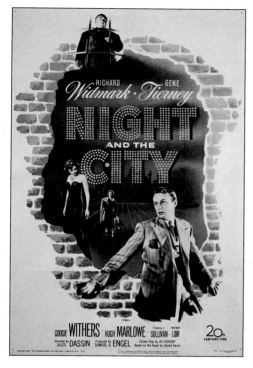

229 NIGHT AND THE CITY, 1950

230 D.O.A., 1950

231 KILL OR BE KILLED, 1950

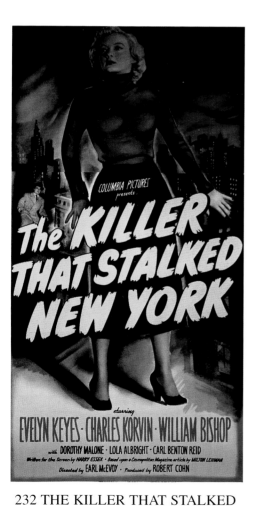

232 THE KILLER THAT STALKED
NEW YORK, 1950, three-sheet

233 GUN CRAZY, 1950, three-sheet

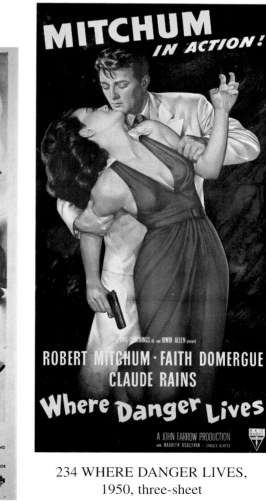

234 WHERE DANGER LIVES,
1950, three-sheet

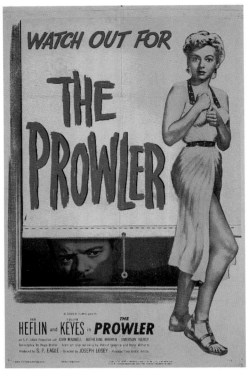

235 THE PROWLER, 1951

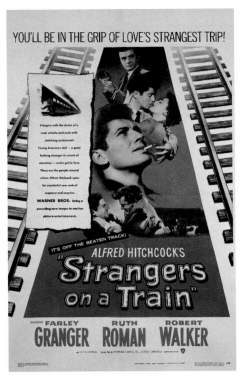

236 STRANGERS ON A TRAIN, 1951

237 A PLACE IN THE SUN, 1951

238 THE LAVENDER HILL MOB, 1951, English poster

239 PICKUP, 1951

240 THE NARROW MARGIN, 1952

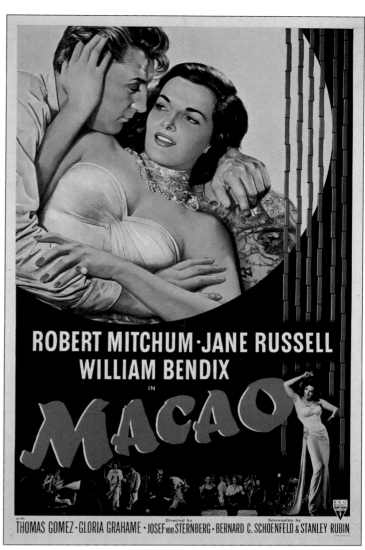

241 MACAO, 1952

242 THE BIG HEAT, 1953

243 DIAL M FOR MURDER, 1954, British quad

244 ON THE WATERFRONT, 1954, lobby card

245 PAID TO KILL, 1954, lobby card

246 BEYOND A REASONABLE DOUBT, 1954

247 NIGHT OF THE HUNTER, 1955, lobby card

248 TO CATCH A THIEF, 1955

249 OVER-EXPOSED, 1956

250 WHILE THE CITY SLEEPS, 1956

251 WITNESS FOR THE PROSECUTION, 1957

252 JAILHOUSE ROCK, 1957

253 REFORM SCHOOL GIRL, 1957

254 TOUCH OF EVIL, 1958

255 VERTIGO, 1958, forty by sixty

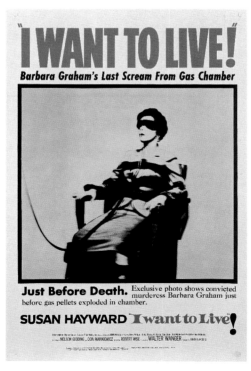

256 I WANT TO LIVE, 1958

257 MACHINE GUN KELLY, 1958

258 THE BONNIE PARKER STORY, 1958

259 CRY BABY KILLER, 1958

260 AL CAPONE, 1959

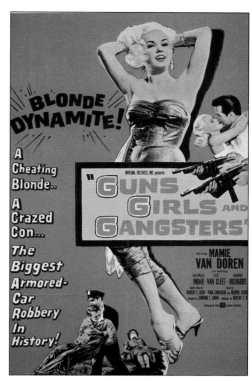

261 GUNS GIRLS AND
GANGSTERS, 1959

262 ANATOMY OF A MURDER, 1959

263 COMPULSION, 1959

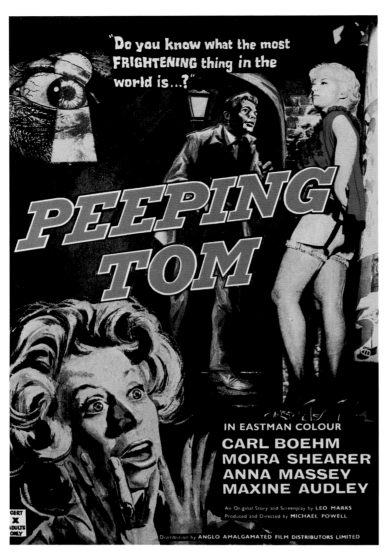

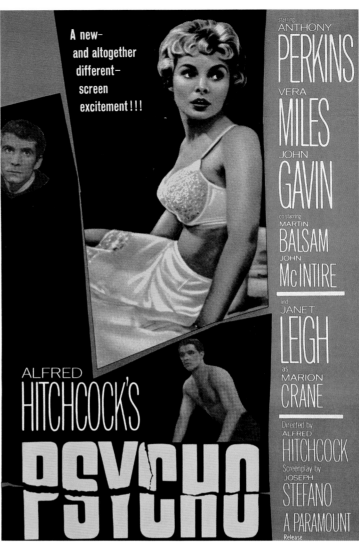

264 PEEPING TOM, 1960

265 PSYCHO, 1960

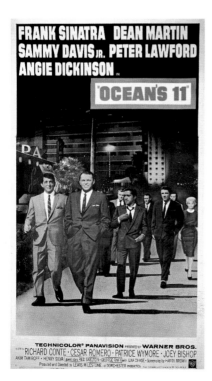

266 OCEAN'S 11, 1960
three-sheet

267 BIRD MAN OF ALCATRAZ, 1962

268 TO KILL A MOCKINGBIRD,
1962

269 CAPE FEAR, 1962

270 CHARADE, 1963

271 STRAIT-JACKET, 1964

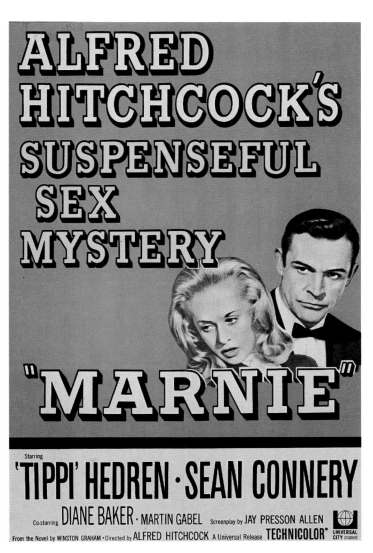

272 MARNIE, 1964

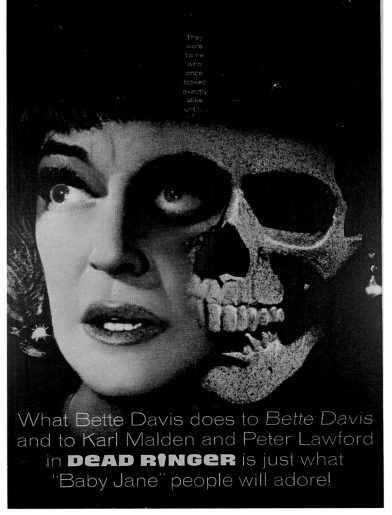

273 DEAD RINGER, 1964

274 HOW TO MURDER YOUR WIFE, 1965

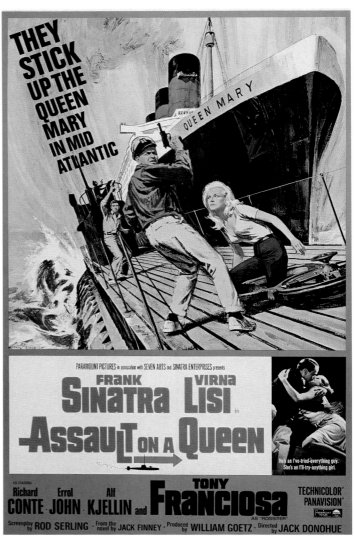

275 ASSAULT ON A QUEEN, 1966

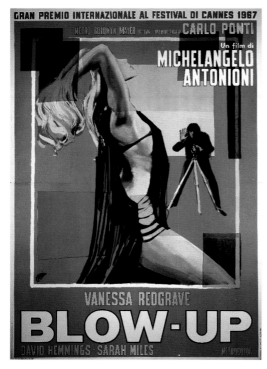

276 BLOW-UP, 1966
Italian poster

277 THE FORTUNE COOKIE, 1966

278 HOW TO STEAL A MILLION,
1966

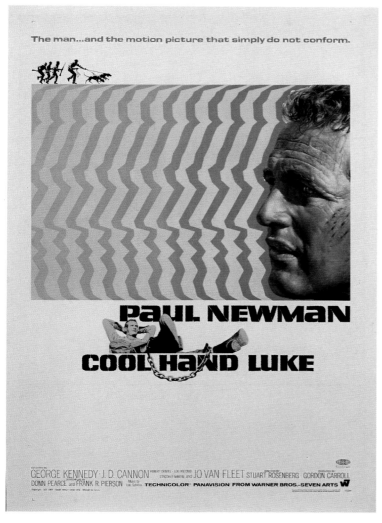

279 COOL HAND LUKE, 1967

280 BONNIE AND CLYDE, 1967
German poster

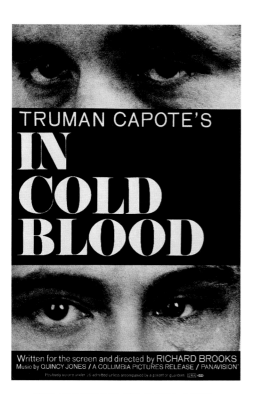

281 IN COLD BLOOD, 1967

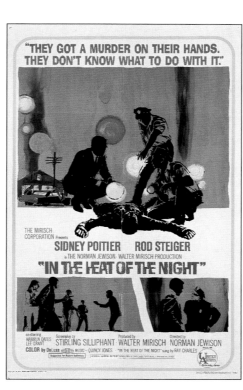

282 IN THE HEAT OF THE NIGHT,
1967

283 POINT BLANK, 1967

284 BULLITT, 1963, German poster

285 COOGAN'S BLUFF, 1968

286 THE THOMAS CROWN
AFFAIR, 1968

287 THE BIGGEST BUNDLE OF
THEM ALL, 1968

288 THE BOSTON STRANGLER,
1968

289 THE NIGHT OF THE
FOLLOWING DAY, 1969

290 BLOODY MAMA, 1970

291 A BULLET FOR PRETTY BOY,
1970

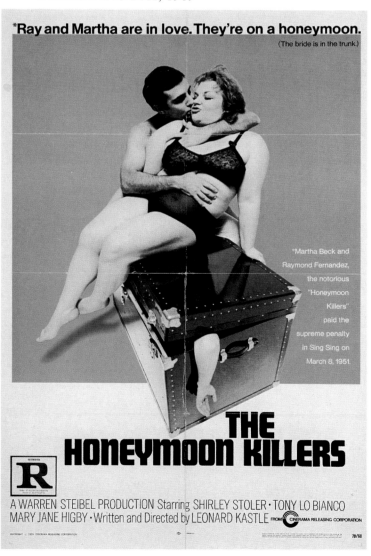

292 THE HONEYMOON KILLERS, 1970

293 COTTON COMES TO HARLEM, 1970

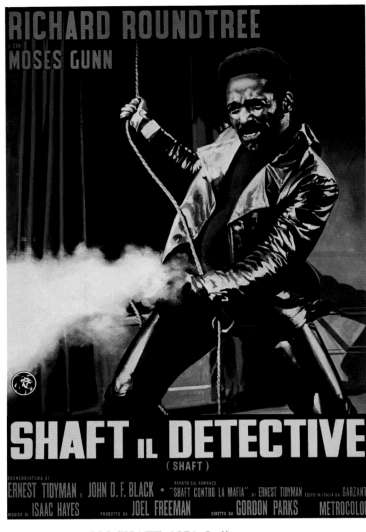

294 DIRTY HARRY, 1970

295 SHAFT, 1971, Italian poster

296 THE FRENCH CONNECTION,
1971

297 KLUTE, 1971

298 PLAY MISTY FOR ME, 1971

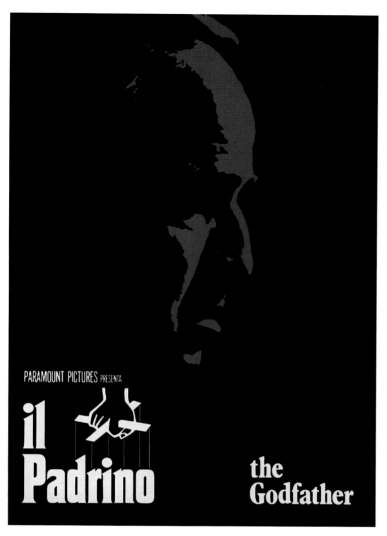

299 THE GODFATHER, 1972, Italian poster

300 THE GETAWAY, 1972

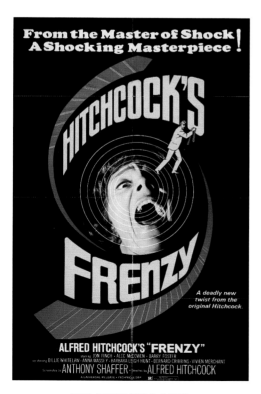

301 FRENZY, 1972

302 THE HOT ROCK, 1972

303 THE GODSON, 1972

304 SLAUGHTER, 1972

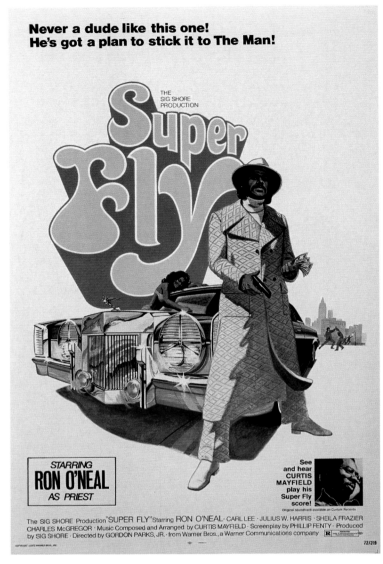

305 SUPER FLY, 1972

306 BLACK MAMA WHITE
MAMA, 1972

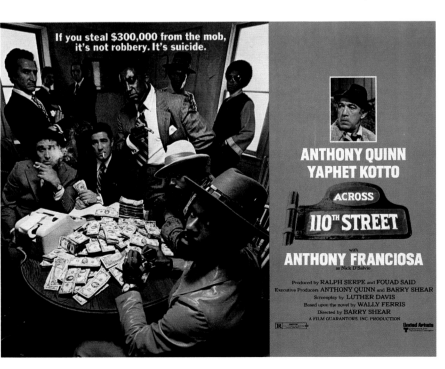

307 ACROSS 110TH STREET, 1972, half-sheet

308 THE STING, 1973,
forty by sixty

309 MAGNUM FORCE, 1973

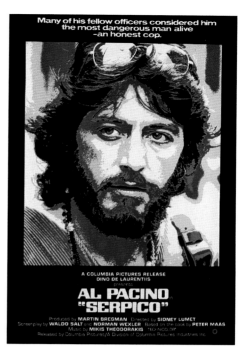

310 SERPICO, 1973

311 THE LONG GOODBYE, 1973

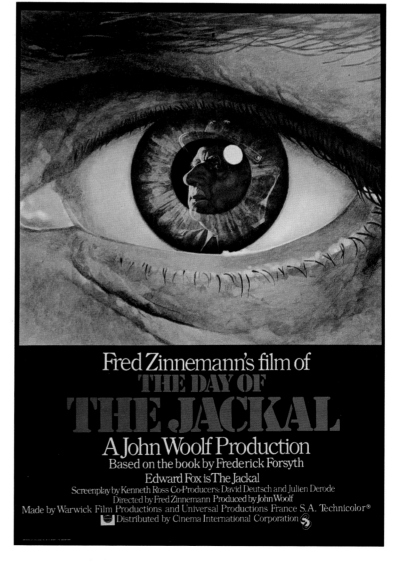

312 THE DAY OF THE JACKAL, 1973

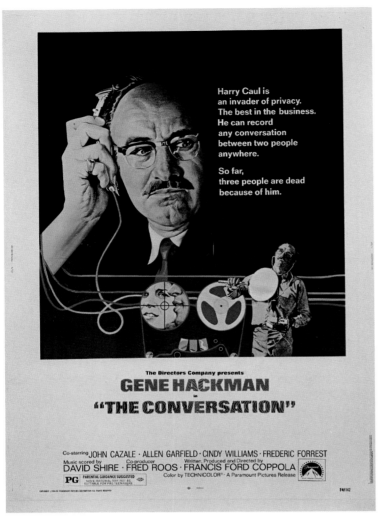

313 THE CONVERSATION, 1974

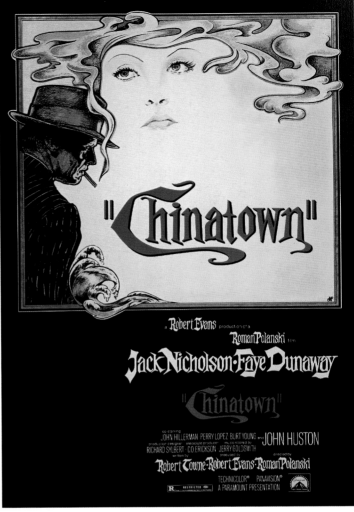

314 CHINATOWN, 1974

315 THIEVES LIKE US, 1974

316 TNT JACKSON, 1974

317 THUNDERBOLT AND
LIGHTFOOT, 1974

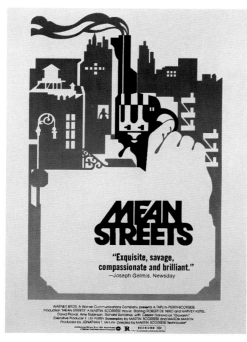

318 MEAN STREETS, 1973

319 BADLANDS, 1974

320 BIG BAD MAMA, 1974

321 THE GODFATHER PART II, 1974

322 THE TAKING OF PELHAM ONE TWO THREE, 1974

323 FAREWELL MY LOVELY, 1975

324 FRIDAY FOSTER, 1975

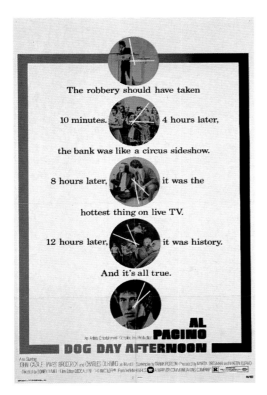

325 DOG DAY AFTERNOON, 1975

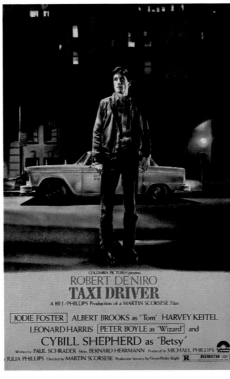

326 TAXI DRIVER, 1976

327 JACKSON COUNTY JAIL, 1976

328 THE GAUNTLET, 1977

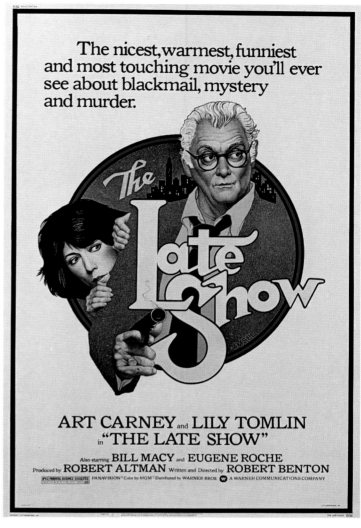

329 THE LATE SHOW, 1977

330 THE BIG SLEEP, 1978

331 FOUL PLAY, 1978

332 MIDNIGHT EXPRESS, 1978

333 MAD MAX, 1979

334 THE LADY IN RED, 1979

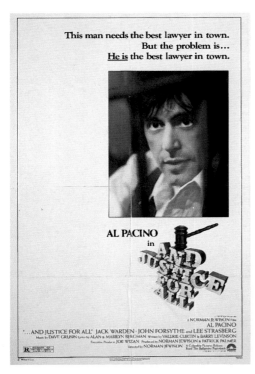

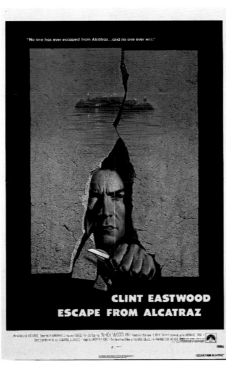

335 AND JUSTICE FOR ALL, 1979

336 ESCAPE FROM ALCATRAZ, 1979

337 STIR CRAZY, 1980

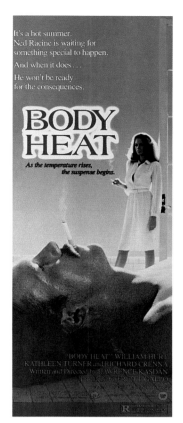

338 ESCAPE FROM NEW YORK, 1981

339 BODY HEAT, 1981,
insert

340 PRINCE OF THE CITY, 1981

341 MS. 45, 1981

342 THE POSTMAN ALWAYS RINGS TWICE, 1981

343 BLADE RUNNER, 1982

344 48 HOURS, 1982

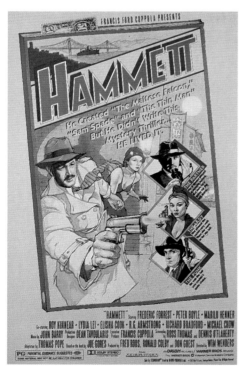

345 HAMMETT, 1982

346 BLOOD SIMPLE, 1983

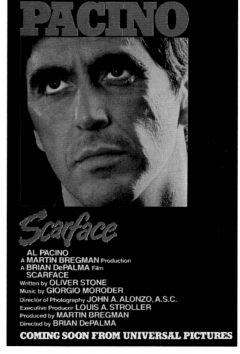

347 SCARFACE, 1983

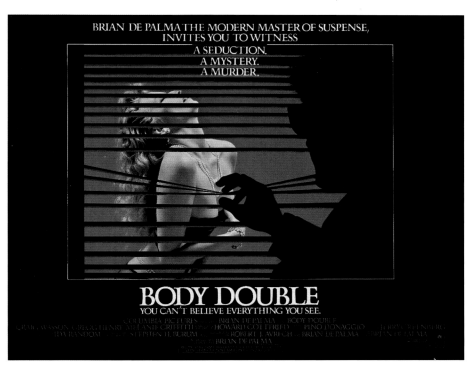

348 BODY DOUBLE, 1984, half-sheet

349 THE COTTON CLUB, 1984

350 PRIZZI'S HONOR, 1985

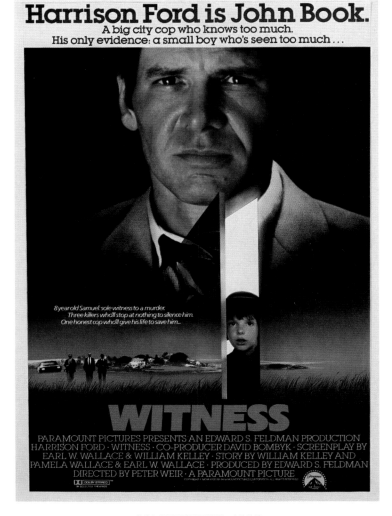

351 WITNESS, 1985

352 MONA LISA, 1986

353 THE BIG EASY, 1987

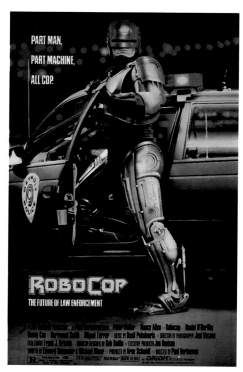

354 ROBOCOP, 1987

355 THE UNTOUCHABLES, 1987

356 THE ACCUSED, 1988

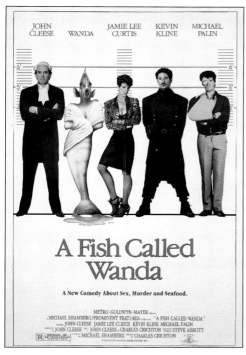

357 A FISH CALLED WANDA, 1988

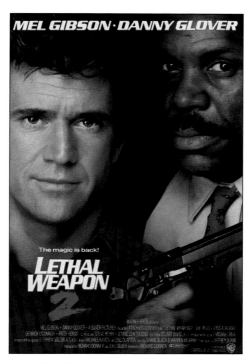

358 LETHAL WEAPON 2, 1989

359 MILLER'S CROSSING, 1989

360 SEA OF LOVE, 1989

361 DICK TRACY, 1990

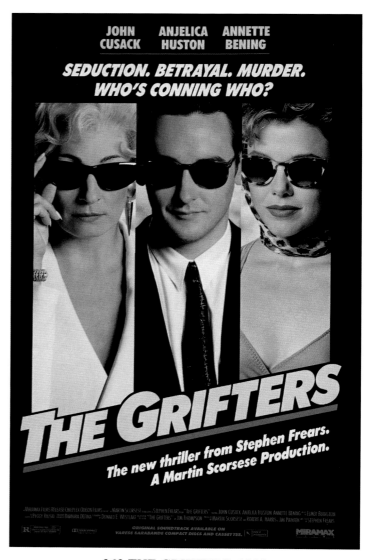

362 GOODFELLAS, 1990

363 THE GRIFTERS, 1990

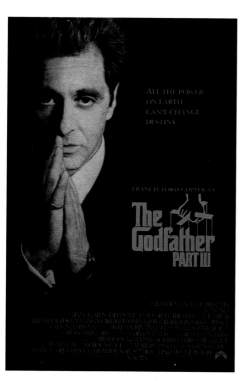

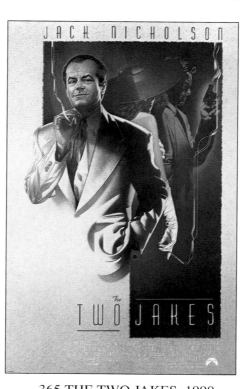

364 THE GODFATHER PART III, 1990

365 THE TWO JAKES, 1990

366 BUGSY, 1991

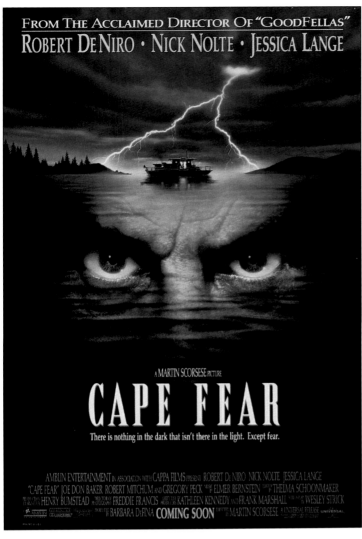

367 CAPE FEAR, 1991

368 THE SILENCE OF THE LAMBS, 1991

369 THELMA AND LOUISE, 1991

370 MY COUSIN VINNY, 1992

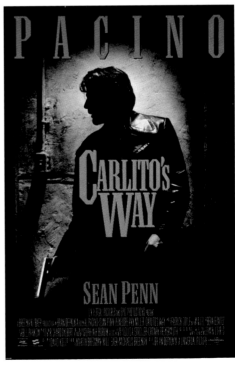

371 CARLITO'S WAY, 1993

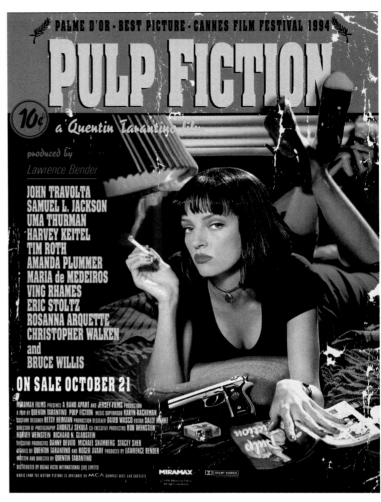

373 PULP FICTION, 1995

372 NATURAL BORN KILLERS, 1995

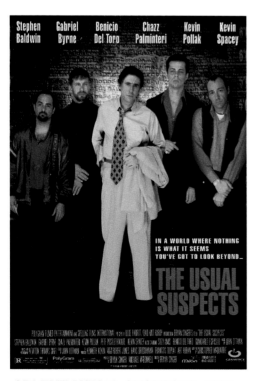

374 THE USUAL SUSPECTS, 1995

375 GANGSTAS, 1996

376 FARGO, 1996

# CRIME MOVIE POSTERS INDEX


THE ACCUSED ... 356
ACROSS 110TH STREET ... 307
THE ADVENTURES OF SHERLOCK HOLMES ... 144
AFTER THE THIN MAN ... 75
AL CAPONE ... 260
ALGIERS ... 112
ALL THROUGH THE NIGHT ... 170
THE AMATEUR DETECTIVE ... 17
THE AMAZING DR. CLITTERHOUSE ... 115
ANATOMY OF A MURDER ... 262
AND JUSTICE FOR ALL ... 335
ANGELS WITH DIRTY FACES ... 103, 104
ARSENE LUPIN ... 53
ASSAULT ON A QUEEN ... 275
THE AVENGING CONSCIENCE ... 2

BADLANDS ... 319
BEYOND A REASONABLE DOUBT ... 246
BIG BAD MAMA ... 320
THE BIG CLOCK ... 220
THE BIG EASY ... 353
THE BIGGEST BUNDLE OF THEM ALL ... 287
THE BIG HEAT ... 242
THE BIG SLEEP (1946) ... 197
THE BIG SLEEP (1978) ... 330
BIRD MAN OF ALCATRAZ ... 267
THE BLACK CAMEL ... 41
BLACK LEGION ... 90
BLACK MAGIC ... 132
BLACKMAIL ... 31
BLACK MAMA WHITE MAMA ... 306
BLADE RUNNER ... 343
BLONDIE JOHNSON ... 63
BLOOD SIMPLE ... 346
BLOODY MAMA ... 290
BLOW-UP ... 276
THE BLUE DAHLIA ... 194
BODY DOUBLE ... 348
BODY HEAT ... 339
BONNIE AND CLYDE ... 280
THE BONNIE PARKER STORY ... 258
BORDERTOWN ... 82
BORN TO KILL ... 209
BOSTON BLACKIE GOES HOLLYWOOD ... 176
THE BOSTON STRANGLER ... 288
BROTHER ORCHID ... 156
BUGSY ... 366
BULLDOG DRUMMOND ... 32
A BULLET FOR PRETTY BOY ... 291
BULLITT ... 284

CALL NORTHSIDE 777 ... 222
THE CANARY MURDER CASE ... 27
CAPE FEAR (1962) ... 269
CAPE FEAR (1991) ... 367
CARLITO'S WAY ... 371
CASABLANCA ... 174
THE CASE OF THE BLACK CAT ... 92
CHARADE ... 270
CHARLIE CHAN AT MONTE CARLO ... 47
CHARLIE CHAN AT THE CIRCUS ... 45
CHARLIE CHAN AT THE OLYMPICS ... 48
CHARLIE CHAN AT THE OPERA ... 46
CHARLIE CHAN AT THE WAX MUSEUM ... 129
CHARLIE CHAN IN SHANGHAI ... 44
CHARLIE CHAN IN THE SECRET SERVICE ... 130
CHARLIE CHAN ON BROADWAY ... 49
CHARLIE CHAN'S CHANCE ... 42
CHARLIE CHAN'S GREATEST CASE ... 43
CHINATOWN ... 314
THE CHINESE CAT ... 131
THE CHINESE RING ... 138
THE CIRCUS QUEEN MURDER ... 65
CITY IN DARKNESS ... 128
COMPULSION ... 263
THE CONVERSATION ... 313
COOGAN'S BLUFF ... 285
COOL HAND LUKE ... 279
THE COTTON CLUB ... 349
COTTON COMES TO HARLEM ... 293
THE CRIME DOCTOR ... 69
CRIME SCHOOL ... 100, 102
CROSSFIRE ... 205
CRY BABY KILLER ... 259
CRY MURDER ... 212
THE CYPHER MESSAGE ... 3

DANGEROUS MONEY ... 135
DARK ALIBI ... 136
DARK PASSAGE ... 202
DARK SHADOWS ... 175
THE DAY OF THE JACKAL ... 312
DEAD END ... 99, 101
DEADLY IS THE FEMALE ... 227
DEAD RECKONING ... 204
DEAD RINGER ... 273
DETOUR ... 188
DEVIL'S CARGO ... 169
THE DEVIL THUMBS A RIDE ... 208
DIAL M FOR MURDER ... 243
DICK TRACY (1937) ... 107, 108
DICK TRACY (1945) ... 109
DICK TRACY (1990) ... 361
DICK TRACY'S DILEMMA ... 111
DICK TRACY VS. CUEBALL ... 110
DILLINGER ... 189
DIRTY HARRY ... 294
D.O.A. ... 230
DOCKS OF NEW ORLEANS ... 139
THE DOCKS OF NEW YORK ... 20
DOG DAY AFTERNOON ... 325
THE DOORWAY TO HELL ... 36
DOUBLE INDEMNITY ... 185
DRESSED TO KILL ... 153

EACH DAWN I DIE ... 126
ESCAPE FROM ALCATRAZ ... 336
ESCAPE FROM NEW YORK ... 338

THE ETERNAL LAW ... 4
THE FALCON AND THE CO-EDS ... 163
THE FALCON IN DANGER ... 164
THE FALCON IN HOLLYWOOD ... 165
THE FALCON IN MEXICO ... 166
THE FALCON OUT WEST ... 167
THE FALCON'S ALIBI ... 168
THE FALCON'S BROTHER ... 160
THE FALCON STRIKES BACK ... 162
THE FALCON TAKES OVER ... 161
FAREWELL MY LOVELY ... 323
FARGO ... 376
THE FEATHERED SERPENT ... 141
A FISH CALLED WANDA ... 357
FORCE OF EVIL ... 214
THE FORTUNE COOKIE ... 277
48 HOURS ... 344
FOUL PLAY ... 331
THE FRENCH CONNECTION ... 296
FRENZY ... 301
FRIDAY FOSTER ... 324

GANGSTAS ... 375
GASLIGHT ... 183
THE GAUNTLET ... 328
THE GAY FALCON ... 159
THE GETAWAY ... 300
GILDA ... 201
THE GIRL, THE COP, THE BURGLAR ... 8
THE GLASS KEY ... 172
G-MEN ... 79
THE GODFATHER ... 299
THE GODFATHER PART III ... 364
THE GODFATHER PART II ... 321
THE GODSON ... 303
GOODFELLAS ... 362
THE GREENE MURDER CASE ... 30
THE GRIFTERS ... 363
GUILTY AS HELL ... 51
GUN CRAZY ... 233
GUNS GIRLS AND GANGSTERS ... 261

HAMMETT ... 345
HELL'S KITCHEN ... 105
HIGH SIERRA ... 158
THE HONEYMOON KILLERS ... 292
THE HONOR OF THE FORCE ... 1
THE HOODLUM ... 12
THE HOT ROCK ... 302
THE HOUND OF THE BASKERVILLES ... 143
THE HOUSE OF FEAR ... 151
HOW TO MURDER YOUR WIFE ... 274
HOW TO STEAL A MILLION ... 278

I AM A CRIMINAL ... 127
I AM A FUGITIVE FROM A CHAIN GANG ... 58-60
I LOVE TROUBLE ... 217
IN COLD BLOOD ... 281
THE INFORMER ... 80
INNER SANCTUM MYSTERY ... 219
IN THE HEAT OF THE NIGHT ... 282
I WALK ALONE ... 206
I WANT TO LIVE ... 256

JACKSON COUNTY JAIL ... 327
JAILHOUSE ROCK ... 252
JEWEL ROBBERY ... 57
JUKE GIRL ... 171

KEY LARGO ... 216
THE KILLERS ... 196
THE KILLER THAT STALKED NEW YORK ... 232
KILL OR BE KILLED ... 231
KING OF CHINATOWN ... 124
KING OF THE UNDERWORLD ... 123
KISS OF DEATH ... 207
KLUTE ... 297
LADIES THEY TALK ABOUT ... 67
THE LADY FROM SHANGHAI ... 218
THE LADY IN RED ... 334
LADY IN THE DEATH HOUSE ... 181
LADY IN THE LAKE ... 195
LADY KILLER ... 66
THE LAST GANGSTER ... 97
THE LATE SHOW ... 329
LAURA ... 184
THE LAVENDER HILL MOB ... 238
THE LEAGUE OF FRIGHTENED MEN ... 95
LEAVE HER TO HEAVEN ... 190
LETHAL WEAPON 2 ... 358
THE LETTER ... 154
LIFE IN JOLIET PENITENTIARY ... 5
LITTLE CAESAR ... 38
THE LITTLE GIANT ... 68
THE LODGER ... 182
THE LONG GOODBYE ... 311

M ... 50
MACAO ... 241
MACHINE GUN KELLY ... 257
MAD MAX ... 333
MAGNUM FORCE ... 309
THE MALTESE FALCON ... 155
MANHATTAN MELODRAMA ... 72
MARKED WOMAN ... 98
MARNIE ... 272
MEAN STREETS ... 318
MIDNIGHT EXPRESS ... 332
MILLER'S CROSSING ... 359
MILLION DOLLAR RANSOM ... 73
MINISTRY OF FEAR ... 180
MR. LUCKY ... 179
MR. WONG, DETECTIVE ... 87
MR. WONG IN CHINATOWN ... 88
MONA LISA ... 352
MORIARTY ... 23
MS. 45 ... 341
MURDER, MY SWEET ... 186
MY COUSIN VINNY ... 370
THE MYSTERIOUS DR. FU MANCHU ... 29
MYSTERIOUS MR. MOTO ... 114
MYSTERIOUS MR. WONG ... 85
THE MYSTERY OF MR. WONG ... 86

NAKED CITY ... 211
THE NARROW MARGIN ... 240
NATURAL BORN KILLERS ... 372
NIGHT AND THE CITY ... 229
THE NIGHT OF THE FOLLOWING DAY ... 289
THE NIGHT OF THE HUNTER ... 247
NOTORIOUS ... 193

OCEAN'S 11 ... 266
ON THE WATERFRONT ... 244
OUT OF THE FOG ... 157
OUT OF THE PAST ... 203
OUTSIDE THE LAW ... 15, 16
OVER-EXPOSED ... 249

PAID TO KILL ... 245
PEEPING TOM ... 264
THE PENALTY ... 13
THE PENGUIN POOL MURDER ... 56
THE PERFECT CRIME ... 21
THE PERILS OF PAULINE ... 11
THE PETRIFIED FOREST ... 93, 94
PHANTOM OF CHINATOWN ... 89
PICKUP ... 239
A PLACE IN THE SUN ... 237
PLAY MISTY FOR ME ... 298
POINT BLANK ... 283
THE POSTMAN ALWAYS RINGS TWICE (1946) ... 200
THE POSTMAN ALWAYS RINGS TWICE (1981) ... 342
PRINCE OF THE CITY ... 340
PRISON WITHOUT BARS ... 116
PRIZZI'S HONOR ... 350
THE PROWLER ... 235
PSYCHO ... 265
THE PUBLIC ENEMY ... 39, 40
PUBLIC HERO NUMBER 1 ... 84
PULP FICTION ... 373

QUIET PLEASE, MURDER ... 177

RAFFLES ... 34
THE RED DRAGON ... 134
REFORM SCHOOL GIRL ... 253
THE RETURN OF SHERLOCK HOLMES ... 26
THE ROARING TWENTIES ... 122
ROBOCOP ... 354
ROPE ... 215

THE SAINT IN NEW YORK ... 117
THE SAINT IN PALM SPRINGS ... 119
THE SAINT MEETS THE TIGER ... 121
THE SAINT STRIKES BACK ... 118
THE SAINT'S VACATION ... 120
SATAN MET A LADY ... 91
SCARFACE (1932) ... 61, 62
SCARFACE (1983) ... 347
THE SCARLET CLAW ... 149
SCARLET STREET ... 192
SEA OF LOVE ... 360
SECRET BEYOND THE DOOR ... 213
SERPICO ... 310
SHADOW OF A DOUBT ... 178
SHADOW OF THE THIN MAN ... 76
SHAFT ... 295
THE SHANGHAI CHEST ... 140
THE SHANGHAI COBRA ... 133
SHERLOCK HOLMES ... 22, 24
SHERLOCK HOLMES AND THE SECRET WEAPON ... 145
SHERLOCK HOLMES AND THE VOICE OF TERROR ... 146
SHERLOCK HOLMES FACES DEATH ... 148
SHERLOCK HOLMES IN WASHINGTON ... 147
SHOW THEM NO MERCY ... 83
THE SIGN OF FOUR ... 25
THE SILENCE OF THE LAMBS ... 368
THE SILENT WITNESS ... 52
SINNER'S HOLIDAY ... 35
THE SIN OF NORA MORAN ... 70
SKY DRAGON ... 142
SLAUGHTER ... 304
SONG OF THE THIN MAN ... 78
SORRY WRONG NUMBER ... 221
SPELLBOUND ... 191
SPIDER WOMAN ... 150
STAR OF MIDNIGHT ... 81
THE STING ... 308
STIR CRAZY ... 337
THE STORY OF TEMPLE DRAKE ... 64
STRAIT-JACKET ... 271
THE STRANGE CASE OF CLARA DEANE ... 54
THE STRANGE LOVE OF MARTHA IVERS ... 198, 199
STRANGERS ON A TRAIN ... 236
SUPER FLY ... 305

THE TAKING OF PELHAM ONE TWO THREE ... 322
TAXI DRIVER ... 326
TERROR BY NIGHT ... 152
THELMA AND LOUISE ... 369
THEY LIVE BY NIGHT ... 224
THEY MADE ME A CRIMINAL ... 106
THEY WON'T BELIEVE ME ... 210
THIEVES LIKE US ... 315
THE THIN MAN ... 74
THE THIN MAN GOES HOME ... 77
THE THIRD DEGREE ... 7
THIS GUN FOR HIRE ... 173
THE THOMAS CROWN AFFAIR ... 286
THUNDERBOLT ... 28
THUNDERBOLT AND LIGHTFOOT ... 317
TNT JACKSON ... 316
TO CATCH A THIEF ... 248
TO KILL A MOCKINGBIRD ... 268
THE TONGUE MARK ... 9
TOO LATE FOR TEARS ... 226
TOUCH OF EVIL ... 254
TRAFFIC IN SOULS ... 10
THE TRAP ... 137
TRAPPED ... 228
TROUBLE IN PARADISE ... 55
THE TWO JAKES ... 365

UNDERWORLD (1927) ... 19
UNDERWORLD (1937) ... 96
THE UNHOLY THREE (1925) ... 18
THE UNHOLY THREE (1930) ... 37
THE UNTOUCHABLES ... 355
THE USUAL SUSPECTS ... 374

VELVET FINGERS ... 14
VERTIGO ... 255

WANTED BY THE POLICE ... 113
WHERE DANGER LIVES ... 234
WHILE THE CITY SLEEPS ... 250
WHITE HEAT ... 225
WHO'S GUILTY? ... 6
WILD BOYS OF THE ROAD ... 71
THE WINDOW ... 223
WITNESS ... 351
WITNESS FOR THE PROSECUTION ... 251
THE WOMAN IN THE WINDOW ... 187
THE WOMAN WHO NEEDED KILLING ... 33

YOU CAN'T GET AWAY WITH MURDER ... 125

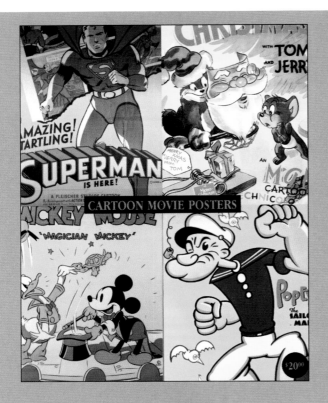

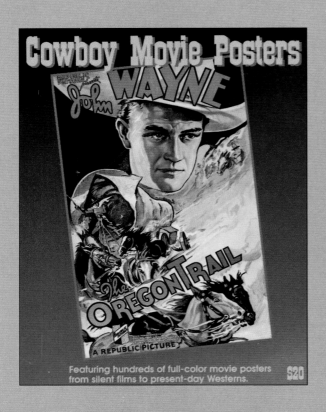

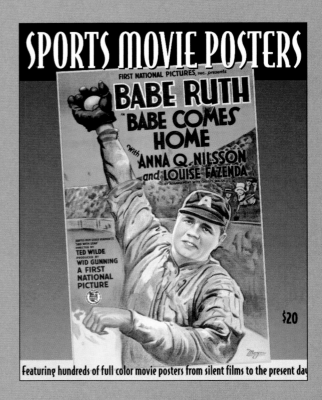